If Wishes
Were Horses:

Proverbs & Stories of
Bernice Bloom Kastner

with recollections by
Judith Skillman, Ruth Kastner and Joel Kastner

BERNICE BLOOM KASTNER

PORTLAND • OREGON
INKWATERPRESS.COM

www.inkwaterpress.com

ISBN-13 978-1-59299-427-4
ISBN-10 1-59299-427-X

Publisher: Inkwater Press

Printed in the U.S.A.
All paper is acid free and meets all ANSI standards for archival quality paper.

1

*To the memory of my mother, whose memoir
"A Letter to My Grandchildren"
showed me how important it is
to leave this kind of record;*

*and to my daughter Judy for suggesting
the use of my "sayings" as a way to
emulate this inspiring example.*

Table of Contents

Foreword ix

1. "An ugly patch is more beautiful than a beautiful hole" 1
2. "If wishes were horses, then beggars would ride" 6
3. "It's an ill wind that blows no good" 9
4. "There's no use crying over spilt milk" 15
5. "If you want something done, give it to a busy
   person" 21
6. "You reap what you sow" 25
7. "You can't be all things to all people" 34
8. "Where there's a will there's a way" 38
9. "A watched pot never boils" 45
10. "Nothing ventured, nothing gained" 49
11. "A thing of beauty is a joy forever" 55
12. "You can curse the darkness or you can light a
    candle" 60
13. "Don't look a gift horse in the mouth" 64
14. "Little children, little problems, big children,
    big problems" 70
15. "April showers bring May flowers" 75
16. "The only constant in life is change" 78
17. "It's like bringing coals to Newcastle" 88
18. "Bit by bit the bowl gets filled" 91

Afterword 95
A Note About Bernice Kastner 98
Contributing Authors 100
Acknowledgements 102

List of Photographs

Photograph 1: Sheyne Rochel and Solomon
    Kestenbaum at Kastner Wedding..................5
Photograph 2: Bernice at age one with her mother
    Leah Bloom................8
Photograph 3: Leah Bloom, with her employees in
    the Inspector Sandwich Shop, circa 1950.................14
Photograph 4: Left to right: Myer, Bernice, and
    Dorothy, with parents Leah and Israel Bloom at
    the Fiftieth Wedding Anniversary Party.................20
Photograph 5: Bernice Kastner, after teaching her
    class at the Takoma Park Campus, Maryland.............24
Photograph 6: Sidney O. Kastner in Syracuse
    Graduate Housing, circa 1955.................32
Photograph 7: Sid and Bernice, dance at their
    wedding, June 30th, 1951, Montreal.................33
Photograph 8: Flyer for Kastner's Kitchen...............48
Photograph 9: Bernice After Her Ph.D Graduation
    Ceremony.................54
Photograph 10: Sid's photo of the total lunar eclipse,
    Virginia Beach, March, 1970.................59
Photograph 11: Sophie Kastner wearing the hat and
    sweater Bernice knit for her.................63
Photograph 12: Bernice featured in the center above
    the school name, as class president.................74
Photograph 13: Photo of "Room 11" 50th reunion
    for Baron Byng High School.................74
Photograph 14: Sid and Bernice visit Mount Rainier,
    September 20, 1998 87

Photograph 15: Bernice with her Greenbelt water
exercise class..94
Photograph 16: Bernice in 1944.................................103
Photograph 17: Bernice with her great grandchildren
Klara June and Hazel Anne Tuininga, 2007.............103

Foreword

--Judith Skillman

When I was growing up, my mother seemed to have a saying for everything that happened—good or bad. I had a difficult childhood, though I was told I was a happy baby by my mother. That happiness, comfort, and ease of life wore off as I became an adolescent in suburban Maryland, attending schools that did not do justice to a creative youngster, and far less to one whose coping skills were woefully maladapted to the diverse world we had entered. My mother attended a school in which the girls and boys had separate classes, and one that was almost wholly Jewish and situated in her own neighborhood; I took a bus to a school whose student body was so diverse it made the term "melting pot" a euphemism for "burning syrup."

The net result of this bizarre difference in our backgrounds was that I became depressed, and when I went to my mother for advice or help she would always listen, give me a bear hug, and tell me she had confidence that I would work out my problems. Perhaps not the best assistance—my insomnia was severe by the time I was thirteen, but better than what some young adults receive from their parents. I did have an excellent role model in mom—she was confident, secure, and she had a technique for allowing sleep to come to her. It had to do with guided imagery. She would pretend she was lying on her back in the water—a lake or pool, and that relaxed her head to toe. In no time she'd be asleep, regardless of what was going on in her life. Our constitutions are very different, and I don't begrudge her rather succinct answers to my severe problems, except I do wish she'd passed on the stamina gene to me!

This collection of my mother's choice proverbs, sayings, witticisms, and aphorisms, and how they relate to her life, reveals a past much different than I imagined it to be as a child. A child or young adult growing up in a family sees that original family only in the context of her or his own limited experience. Both my parents came from strong Jewish backgrounds, yet they raised me more with science and analytic skills at the center of the universe, rather than the Old Testament God. I respect their decision, conscious or unconscious, to do this. The rift it created, however, made me wonder if sometimes I was going insane, growing up so differently than my peers, who had Christmas, and, for the most part, went to church or did not, but had the 'goyim' holidays, and, from my knothole, a more carefree and happy go lucky existence than I did.

One thing I remember my mother saying in particular, and using a lot, when I came to her with my myriad troubles was "If wishes were horses, then beggars would ride." This cuts to the quick of many a child's deepest yearning for the imaginary, rosy world that adults know does not exist. Perhaps I wish she hadn't said it with such certainty. I would try to puzzle it out, and the puzzlement would become a profound confusion: what I want is not a horse, therefore, somewhere in the world, there is a poor person, a beggar, who can't ride off into the sunset. I really tried to fit my imagination around this proverb, to no avail.

After all, what is more important than wishing that things might be different, sharing in the idealism of youthful energy and disappointment it engenders? But all in all, and now that I am in my fifties and have three lovely, grown-up children, I see in the seeds of her wisdom what she herself has reaped, and I say this to my children and to myself, to my own chagrin, much more often than I would ever have expected.

Here, then, are the many and varied aphorisms that belong to Bernice, a woman who chose natural childbirth in the fifties and sixties, when it was not in vogue, a woman ahead of her time—the only woman physics major in her class at McGill University in Montreal. Here, within the delightful nuggets of her proverbs, are the telling stories of her past. Enjoy!

1. "An ugly patch is more beautiful than a beautiful hole"

A myeseh latteh is shener vie a sheyne lokh.

I must have been about ten years old when my grandmother came to live with us after my grandfather died. This caused a huge change in our lives, because my mother was the person who knew the most about our grandfather's business, and the end result was that she took over the management of the business, and my grandmother took over the household. I remember my mother saying that you can't have two cooks in one kitchen, though she used a more colorful Yiddish expression to convey this meaning (which would translate as "you can't have two behinds at one stove").

My grandmother taught me to darn socks, and at first I didn't do a very good job – the origin of the comment at the top – but she also used this expression in a more profound way to teach me about preserving things that are still usable even though they don't look as pretty as they used to.

I have strong memories of going with my grandmother to the local market on Friday afternoons, where she would pick out a live chicken. We had to wait while the *schochet* performed the ritual slaughter, then we would bring the chicken home, where she would spread newspapers on the kitchen table and eviscerate the chicken, separating out the edible parts before disposing of the rest of the innards. It was always exciting to see if there were unhatched eggs, which would be cooked briefly at the end when she boiled the chicken for our Sabbath meal.

Either my sister or I had to accompany my grandmother to help carry all the food she bought at the market in addition to the chicken – we still had an icebox in those days, and did not keep a big store of food that needed refrigeration. She also wanted one of us available during the evisceration process, in case she saw something in the chicken's innards that she thought might not be kosher. When this happened, thankfully on rare occasions, she would wrap everything up in layers of newspaper and I would be sent off to have it inspected by the sage who lived a block or so away and made such rulings. I don't remember ever being told that we couldn't eat that chicken.

There were a number of accommodations we were forced to make as a result of having my grandmother join our household, not least of which was that she had to sleep in the bedroom my sister and I shared, but the biggest casualty for me was that after a year or so of struggle I gave up my piano lessons. It seemed that every time I practiced my grandmother would say that it was giving her a headache (*"es klapt in kop"*). My sister was more stubborn, she fought more with our grandmother and persisted with her piano lessons.

When my grandmother had lived with us for about seven years, I came home from school one afternoon and she wasn't home. I was in my last year in high school by then, and carried a key, and I thought she must have gone out to get something for dinner. A short time later she arrived, carrying nothing but her purse, sat down in the living room and burst into tears. I was astounded – until then the only time I had seen her cry was when my grandfather had died. I asked her what was wrong, and she wiped her eyes and responded with a question of her own: "Look at me, don't you see something different?" It would have taken someone who paid much more attention to detail than I did to see the difference, and she had to show me that she was wearing new earrings.

I was also supposed to understand the deep significance of this, which she patiently explained while she delivered her bombshell. The previous earrings had been given to her by my grandfather when they married, and she was wearing the new ones (that really didn't look much different) because she had a new husband!! Apparently her new husband, also widowed, had been using a network of relatives and a marriage broker to seek a new wife, and he had chosen my grandmother. It may be worth noting that my grandmother's given name was *"Sheyne Rochel"* (Beautiful Rachel) and she was indeed still very nice-looking. The community also knew that she was devout and a good cook, both important to Solomon Kestenbaum, her new husband.

It seems that Mr. Kestenbaum had arranged to come for her in a taxi and she thought they were going to visit his daughter. Instead he had brought her to the home of a Rabbi, who took Sheyne Rochel into his study and told her that Mr. Kestenbaum wanted to marry her, that there was an assemblage of men waiting in another room so that the ceremony could be legal in the eyes of God. Then he said she had to decide, yes or no. She said "maybe" but he told her that only a yes or no would be acceptable. I didn't ask how long she thought about it before she said yes. Then her new husband took her to our home to break the news to the family that she was moving to the town of Smith Falls in Ontario with her new husband, although he did not accompany her inside.

Interestingly enough, it was a very happy marriage. When my husband and I moved from Ottawa to Syracuse so that he could start graduate school, it was convenient to travel via Smith Falls and pay them a visit. She knew we were coming, but when we arrived nobody was home. However a few minutes later a truck drove up, Mr. Kestenbaum at the wheel and Sheyne Rochel – whom I had always known as a very queasy rider in a car - sitting in the passenger seat, her arm on the window ledge, looking comfortable and happy. She made tea, served us her wonderful strudel, and we had a pleasant visit. I had a few moments alone with her before we left, and I asked if she was happy. She said she was very happy, and that the only thing she might wish for now was to be ten years younger!

**Sheyne Rochel and Solomon Kestenbaum
at Kastner Wedding**

2. "If wishes were horses, then beggars would ride"

I must have heard my mother say this many times when I was very young. I feel as though I always understood that she was telling me that if I wanted something to happen, I needed to do something other than wish for it.

My mother was a great believer in the idea that children learned to make decisions by seeing that they were expected to do so, that they learned responsibility by being given responsibility, and that they learned to manage money by having money to manage. I know I was the only one among my friends who had a clothing allowance at the age of twelve.

At that time, my father was working in the ladies clothing industry as a cutter and designer of coats and suits. Whenever my sister or I outgrew a coat, he enjoyed designing a new one for whichever girl needed one – or for both of us, so they would match -- and then he would cut it from the remnants of cloth that were available to him. The factory owner allowed one of the seamstresses to sew the child-size garments, so this meant that I always had a nice coat – important in a city as cold as Montreal – that I didn't have to buy.

We wore uniforms to school, and these were bought at the beginning of each school year, which meant that my monthly clothing allowance was designed to cover the cost of whatever clothing I would need for purposes other than school, and for necessities like underwear and pajamas. It was made very clear to me when the clothing allowance was started that if I did not plan carefully and I needed something to wear but had no money left, I should expect to wait until the next month. If I wanted or needed something that cost more than a single month's allowance, it was also made clear that I would have to save for this.

These rules that were set down were observed strictly, and my mother was the enforcer of these rules. It was only after I was grown and earning my own money that I realized that my father was actually the keeper of the family purse, and that he probably would have allowed more leeway. But it would never have occurred to me to discuss this with him, he made it clear that all of this was my mother's domain.

It was when my parents visited while I was already married, in graduate school and receiving a stipend for teaching, that the reality of my father's control of the family finances came through to me, because my mother expressed her joy when she observed that I had my own bank account. I had always seen my father as generous, and I think it's true that he was far more generous than most men in his financial position would have been. What I did not understand until that moment was the issue of control as it appeared to my mother. At this point in their lives my parents were in business together, and they both were working very long hours, making a living but with not much to spare, and she clearly felt she was not in a position to make decisions that were important to her.

Bernice at age one with her mother Leah Bloom

3. "It's an ill wind that blows no good"

I grew up in an atmosphere of optimism and with the feeling that we each have it in us to overcome adversity. My father was a very short man, probably about 5'2" tall. I once heard him say that he had over trained in gymnastics in his youth, and that this had stunted his growth, but in general everyone took him as he was, himself included, and he always seemed able to see the bright side of things.

He was the oldest child, with three siblings, in a family that emigrated from Russia to Montreal when he was about thirteen. We never actually knew his age, because his mother didn't want anyone to extrapolate her age by knowing his, but my mother said he must have been born in 1900, give or take a year. The family had left Russia (actually the Ukraine) after four or five agonizing years of keeping the youngest member of the family, his brother Ben, hidden in their basement, or, if they had to take him out, dressed as a girl. This was because if the local authorities had learned there was another male child in this family, the older boy – my father – would have been taken as a conscript in the Tsar's army.

While growing up in Russia, my father trained seriously in gymnastics, and I recall seeing him perform as part of the YMHA gymnastics team. He also liked to entertain his children, later his grandchildren, by walking on his hands, which he was able to keep up for several minutes. He was always physically fit, and when he developed high blood pressure late in life, he stepped up his physical fitness routine and did not have to take medication to control hypertension for very long.

He arrived in Montreal at the age of about thirteen speaking no English, and he never lost his Russian accent, but he studied on his own and took the Provincial Matriculation Examinations and qualified to enter McGill University. Of course, the family could not afford this, and for a while he helped in the family business until he entered a trade and became a cutter in a ladies' garment factory. He also took courses in design, and I remember seeing him sketch coats and suits when I was very young.

My father's family was very Orthodox, but this was not his view of life; he was more interested in science and philosophy and felt that religion was not a good basis for decisions about his life. He rarely engaged in arguing about these issues, or about anything else, for that matter. He simply let everyone have his or her say, and then he quietly did whatever he wanted to. He had no tolerance for complaints or whining – his response if you expressed unhappiness or dissatisfaction to him was "Snap out of it."

On the other hand, he was also supportive of others' needs to do what was important to them. When my sister had just graduated from high school, she was eighteen years old and wanted to go meet her boyfriend Julio's family in Caracas, Venezuela. Julio and his twin brother Jose were living with an aunt on our street, and had been attending the local high school. My mother was strongly opposed to the idea of letting her youngest child make this trip, but she reported to me many years later that my father persuaded her by arguing: "Do you want to lose your daughter? This is something she intends to do whether or not we support it, and we should help her do it."

My Dad was an excellent chess player, and there was always one chessboard in a corner of our living room where the game he was playing by mail was displayed. He would wait until his opponent's move arrived in the mail, then he would study the board, make his own move and mail it out. He was a patient man!

I always thought of him as not being terribly sociable, because he was not usually an active participant in the chatter at the many family gatherings that took place as I was growing up, but when he and my mother retired and began spending a few months in Miami Beach every winter, he became a raconteur, to everyone's surprise. On the occasion of what we thought was a surprise party for my parents' 50th wedding anniversary, after the toast to this long-standing marriage was made and my parents were called upon to say something, it was my father who pulled some notes out of his pocket and gave a most entertaining speech.

One of my most cherished memories of my father is of an occasion not long after we discovered how well I had done in the Provincial Matriculation Exams when I graduated from high school. We were alone together a week or so later, and he said to me: "You know, kid, you can do anything you want to." Several months afterwards, as my first year at McGill University was far enough along that I had to make a decision about what kind of major to choose, I decided to apply for the Honours Mathematics and Physics program. My mother was opposed to this idea, as she thought I would be jeopardizing my marriage opportunities ("Boys don't like a girl to be too smart"). My father did not participate in the discussion, as was common, but he was there and I stood my ground – after all, he had told me I could do anything I wanted to! Also, I had earned a good scholarship as a result of my standing in the Matriculation Exams, and my parents did not have to pay much tuition for my University education. This made it easier for me to satisfy my own interests, though I was well aware that they were still supporting me.

When I applied for the program, I was invited to the office of the Chairman of the Physics Department, who told me that I would not be accepted. He explained that it was highly unlikely that I would ever be a physicist, and it would be a waste of resources for the department to provide my education in this direction. I borrowed a page from my father's book and did not engage in an argument, I just waited to see how they intended to keep me out. The only way would have been if any of my grades in the science courses had not been "Firsts" but I did have good grades and I did get in.

There were many ironies in this situation, but I will name just two of them:

1. This program had a policy of making one course each year inordinately difficult in order to "weed out" the class. In this 3-year program, there were 40 the first year, 20 the second year, and there were 10 of us who actually graduated with Honours in Mathematics and Physics.

2. Two of the 10 that did graduate never had any intention of becoming physicists – they were in the program because they believed (correctly, as it turned out) that this would help them get into medical school. Both these men were Jewish, and there was a quota for Jews in each entering class at McGill's School of Medicine.

**Leah Bloom, with her employees in the
Inspector Sandwich Shop, circa 1950**

4. "There's no use crying over spilt milk"

It took me a long time to understand that one of the most common emotions that most people have is the feeling of guilt. I still think I really don't know what it feels like, though I've learned to recognize when it seems to be driving people I know. Of course, there have been many times in my life when I have regretted things I've done and wished I'd known better than to do them, but my sense is that this is not the same as feeling guilty because I also feel that in hindsight, if I'd known at the time what I know now, I would not have done whatever it was I regret.

Both my parents seemed to have an attitude that when you make mistakes, the most important thing you can do is learn from them. I think I can speak for my brother and sister when I say that we never felt it was bad to make a mistake, that what was important was to understand what went wrong. I know I had a most idyllic childhood. There was very little money, but my friends, most of whom undoubtedly had more, thought we were rich. I was born in 1931, and the early part of my life was spent in the years of the "Great Depression" but my father kept his job throughout that time, and while it was by no means very much money, my parents certainly seemed to make it go far.

My father did not have a car until I was at University, nor did he buy a house until long after I was married and living in Maryland. However we went out to dinner almost every Saturday, usually just to the deli for smoked meat sandwiches, but occasionally for steak, and eventually we also learned to appreciate Chinese food, though my mother did worry that it might contain pork. My father would say that once a week my mother needed a break from cooking. We also spent every summer "in the country," and those summers were incredibly wonderful.

Most of my friends also left the city for the summer, and in general the families went to resort towns in the Laurentian Mountains north of Montreal, and the fathers came out for the weekends. In my memory we did this once, when I was five years old and recovering from my bout with rheumatic fever, but once was enough for my father to know that he was not happy being with his wife and family only on the weekends. My father was also an avid fisherman and he explored the area called Woodlands on the south shore of the St. Laurence River, where the river broadened out to form Lake St. Louis, and which at that time was mostly farmland.

My parents rented a large farmhouse, and we used it every summer for over 10 years along with three or four other families of aunts, uncles and cousins. The owner, a farmer who spoke only French, moved his family to a smaller "summer" house he had built. In fact the farmer's family – there were two children, younger than we were – never used the whole of the large farmhouse, because the only heat came from the large wood-burning kitchen stove. In the winters, the entire family slept in the large loft room above the kitchen and in the summers he rented the house to city people.

My father would rent a rowboat for the summer – eventually he bought an outboard motor – and every weekend he would catch a lot of fish that the horde of relatives who occupied the house all enjoyed eating. We children would dig for worms, and we all learned how to bait a hook and how to get the fish we caught off the hook. We also learned to swim and row a boat, and enjoyed many a campfire on the stony riverbank.

The only running water in the farmhouse was the pump mounted at the kitchen sink, which we operated by moving the handle up and down. We had no bathroom, there was an outhouse for the toilet and we bathed in the lake. There was also a big wooden tub that was used on very rare occasions, if someone needed to have a warm bath. Unless the weather was very hot, the wood-burning stove always had a fire going, and it was easy enough to heat water – the work was in using the pump to get the water!

What made the summers so idyllic for the children

was being with our cousins. My parents seemed to be the "glue" that united both branches of the family. One of my father's sisters had married a man from New York City, where she lived with her two children who were the same age as my brother and me. They spent every summer with us, and my father's younger sister and her husband, who had two boys a little younger were always with us as well. My mother's younger brother, Louis, and his wife and their three girls also shared the farmhouse.

My mother had five brothers but no sisters, and three of her brothers also lived in Montreal during the period of the Woodlands summers. Her oldest brother, Max and his wife, Malka, had six grown children when I was young, and some of these cousins, along with their families, also rented houses for the summer close by. My cousins Rose and Mary taught me to knit the summer when I was 7, a craft I have enjoyed all my life. They were young mothers, always present and able to help me fix my mistakes when I was just a beginner; they also taught me how to fix them myself once I had mastered the basics. My mother could knit, but Rose and Mary were more enthusiastic about this.

We often had other visitors for short periods during those summers in Woodlands. I will never forget the excitement the summer after World War II ended, when our cousin Sylvia arrived from England in her Air Force Women's Auxiliary uniform. Sylvia was the older daughter of my mother's brother Sol, who had brought Leah and Louis to Canada after their parents died within 6 months of each other. Sol and Dinah had then been married only a short time and they decided to join Sol's older brothers, Max and Joe, in Montreal and brought the two youngest siblings with them. For 14-year-old Leah, this was the first time she had ever met her two oldest brothers. When her parents left Poland to move to Liverpool in England, Max and Joe did not accompany the family but were sent to Canada in the charge of other relatives. My grandparents took the two younger boys, Sol and Harry, to Liverpool with them, and Leah and Louis were born in Liverpool.

Sol and Dinah had two daughters, Sylvia and Evelyn, while they lived in Montreal. The family returned to England while the girls were quite young, so when Sylvia appeared in Woodlands I had never met her. She had served in the women's auxiliary of the Air Force, and because she was born in Canada, she was eligible to enroll in the Canadian service and be demobilized in Canada. Her parents and sister soon joined her in Montreal.

My father's brother Ben and his wife Lillian also spent a week or so with us most summers. Uncle Ben and Aunt Lillian seemed to have a very glamorous life, to my young eyes. They had no children, and they had homes in New York City and Miami Beach. Aunt Lillian was a model and Uncle Ben was a bartender in first class hotels. In summer he worked in a resort hotel in the Laurentian Mountains north of Montreal, and in winter he was at one of the most well-known Miami Beach Hotels. Aunt Lillian modeled women's fashions in New York in the fall and spring, and in the winter she often appeared in fashion shows at one of the elegant department stores in Miami Beach.

When they visited, they often had surprise gifts for the children. One year we were presented with individual copies of a photograph of Danny Kaye taken with my Uncle Ben behind the bar, each copy signed personally by Danny Kaye and bearing an inscription. Mine said "To my friend Bernice" above the signature. Another time there was a box of Canadian quarters and half-dollars, which Uncle Ben had accumulated from tips left for him at the bar that he gave to the three of us to share.

Left to right: Myer, Bernice, and Dorothy, with parents Leah and Israel Bloom at the Fiftieth Wedding Anniversary Party

5. "If you want something done, give it to a busy person"

I do remember when my mother started saying this – I must have been at University at the time. She was an avid reader, and she found a theory about this idea in something she had read, and adopted it enthusiastically. My mother was one of the most educated people I knew, and it was almost entirely self-education. Her formal schooling stopped after grade 8, and she was orphaned at the age of 14. Her mother died of cancer when she was 13, and her father of lung disease about 6 months later. She had asthma herself, and it was her lungs that failed at the end, but she lived a strong and independent life and when she died at the age of 90 the entire family was in shock.

When my mother embraced the idea that busy people are more likely to get things done, she explained that this was because busy people learn how to organize their tasks and their time and become more efficient. Both my parents had prodigious energy, which they took for granted, so this requirement for getting things done did not enter into her analysis of the issue. I've also been fortunate to have a high energy level, though I always felt my parents could run circles around me.

I think it was my exposure to this philosophy, along with the fact that I had been given responsibilities at an early age, that led me to be open to taking on extra duties once I was in my professional life. When I joined the mathematics faculty at Montgomery College, a community college, I was approached by the Learning Resources Department to work with them on a proposal to the National Science Foundation (NSF) under a new program that included projects at two-year colleges.

Although I was new to the job, and still working on my Ph.D. thesis – I had completed the basic work, but there was a lot of writing still to be done – I was intrigued by what appeared to be an opportunity to alleviate a problem endemic in teaching mathematics at the post-secondary level. Different students lack different skills and/or understandings that are needed and assumed available to the students when they have to learn new, more advanced or more abstract mathematics, or when they are studying other sciences like physics and chemistry.

Our proposal to the NSF was funded, and the Mathematics Skills Center at the Rockville campus of Montgomery College was born. In the three years of the project, we produced a set of diagnostic and achievement tests for specific mathematical skills, a catalog of instructional materials geared to these skills, and an administrative system to provide individual help to students who needed it.

During the second year of this project, I experienced an unusual health problem that was ultimately given a name: Benign Positional Vertigo. It simply meant that at completely unpredictable intervals, I would experience very brief episodes of extreme dizziness. This would not have been a real problem—the episodes were indeed very brief—if I had not had to drive to work on the Capital Beltway. Using public transportation took close to two hours each way—there was not yet a metro system in the Washington D.C. area. With the help of some of my colleagues, I stayed on at the Rockville campus until the project was finished, and then was able to transfer to the Takoma Park campus, which was more accessible by public transportation.

As soon as my responsibility to the project was over, I was no longer available to supervise the Center. The department then picked up the ball and the Center flourished. During the development process, those of us working with the project had often wished to see more participation from our colleagues, but it seemed that they didn't see this as necessary until there was a vacuum at the top.

**Bernice Kastner, after teaching her class at
the Takoma Park Campus, Maryland**

6. "You reap what you sow"

This expression is most commonly used in its negative connotation, that you have to live with the result of doing something you should not have done. There is also a positive interpretation, though, which is that when you work hard at something you get to enjoy the benefits of that hard work.

I think this is a good context in which to discuss my marriage. Sid and I had a lot in common, but we had vastly different views of life and completely opposite personalities. When we met, I was outgoing, full of confidence, and serenely oblivious to emotional distress. Sid, on the other hand, was shy, exquisitely sensitive, and had grown up in an atmosphere of conflict and insecurity. He was, however, an excellent communicator, at least with me, and we both worked hard at our relationship and made it succeed.

I would probably have met Sid because my family

moved into the same apartment building in Snowdon at the beginning of my third year at McGill, my second year in the Math & Physics program. In fact, the first time I noticed him was on the day we moved in, when I did not yet have a key and I had to wait outside because I had arrived a bit earlier than the appointed time. He happened to come out of the building as I waited, but a few weeks later I saw him again at a meeting of the McGill Physical Society.

He was a year ahead of me in the program – his final year – and we did not have any classes together. But a group of us left that meeting and started traveling towards our homes on the same bus. I was the only female, of course, and we had animated conversations about the meeting content -- so much for my mother's concern that studying math and physics would impair my chances for marriage. In fact, as the only woman among all those men, if anything it had to enhance them!

One by one, various members of our conversation group got off the bus. New to the neighborhood in which I now lived, I did not realize that day what the simplest route home was, and I got off that bus and transferred to another one while Sid stayed on it. By the next meeting, I had figured it out, and we found ourselves walking together to the very same building!

Sid was very shy and reserved, but both of us had again found the meeting stimulating, and it was natural to talk about it. This was the icebreaker, and we soon found that we shared a lot of interests. Sid must have told his sister Bess about me, because she held a party, and he invited me to come. He had two older brothers as well, both married. Jake was a nuclear physicist who worked at the National Research Council in Ottawa, while Aaron was a Medical Resident at the Jewish General Hospital in Montreal. Sid and Bess and their parents had only recently moved to Montreal from Toronto, where they had spent about three years after Sid's father had lost his position as a Cantor at a Synagogue in Winnipeg.

Sid's father was now established as the Cantor at the Spanish and Portuguese Synagogue in Montreal, but I did not meet him at Bess's party, though I did meet my future mother-in-law there, and apparently I had all the right reactions to win her heart on the spot. I learned later that she had been instructed to keep out of sight, but at one point, when I was returning from a trip to the bathroom, she came out of a bedroom, said hello, told me she was Bess's mother, and asked me in Yiddish what my name was. Since she had asked the question in Yiddish, I replied with my Hebrew name, *Chaieh Broche*, and after that I could do no wrong in her eyes!

I would see Sid every so often around the Physics building, and shortly after the party he asked me to a movie. Thus began our courtship – there was a strong sexual attraction from the start, and in our day and age, I don't think either of us thought of any way other than marriage to respond to this. We met in September, Bess had her party in November or December, by March we became engaged, and we were married at the end of June. I had just turned 20 the previous May.

The summer of my marriage, I had a wonderful job in Ottawa at the National Research Council of Canada (NRC), doing measurements and calculations for scientists that today would all be done by computer. For example, I did wind tunnel measurements on models of jet planes under development, and I used an instrument called a planimeter to measure areas enclosed by curves that came out of experiments. Meanwhile, Sid had a job in the infrared physics group at NRC. I stayed with Sid's brother Jake's family until we were married, and we found a nice little apartment for the rest of that summer.

As the summer drew to an end, Sid was planning to continue in his job, and I was most reluctant to return to Montreal to complete my degree, but Sid insisted. He told me that his conscience would not allow him to feel that because of him I had forsaken my education, and he pointed out that it would only take eight months, and that we could be together every weekend. With only one salary, though, we could not afford to keep the apartment in Ottawa, but Sid said that he didn't need to have a kitchen, and he rented a room in the home of a retired couple.

Shortly after I started my final year at McGill, Dorothy and Julio decided to get married. This presented a new problem, because Dorothy and Julio were both fresh out of high school, and it was clear that they could not yet afford to have their own apartment. Dorothy and I shared a room in my parents' two-bedroom apartment – Myer was away in graduate school in Urbana, Illinois – and it was my mother-in-law who came up with the obvious solution. The Kastners had bought a house, and she pointed out that they had Sid's room, and that clearly I should live with them and let Dorothy and Julio use the bedroom in my parents' apartment.

This is what we did, and I soon began to understand that until then I had lived in an extremely sheltered world compared to most people, and certainly compared to Sid. My mother-in-law was an unusual person, generally described by people who knew her as "difficult." She had absolutely no housekeeping skills, but she could not keep any household help because she was suspicious of them and accused them of stealing whenever she could not find something that she herself had mislaid.

On the other hand, she was the opposite of the traditional Jewish mother-in-law who is convinced that no woman is good enough for her sons – I remember her telling me that any woman who was smart enough to marry one of her sons was obviously very smart and therefore worthy. She herself had been very well educated in Poland, she spoke several languages, had studied philosophy, was familiar with German literature, and wrote poetry in the Polish language which had been published. Her father had been the village notary, and she had been his assistant until she married, since he had no sons. She was thrilled with the fact that I was at University and she let me know that she thought I was wonderful.

She was, however, not happy in her marriage. It had been an arranged marriage, and her parents had forced her into it so that her younger sister could marry. In their culture, it was considered disgraceful for a younger sister to marry while the older one was single. To make matters even worse, my father-in-law had a large family – there were nine siblings – and she endured scorn and ridicule from her husband's family because she could neither cook nor keep house.

I found my father-in-law to be easy-going and pleasant, but Sid perceived his father as uncommunicative and distant, while he saw his mother as volatile and unreliable. I know there were many conflicts in the home when the children were young, and my mother-in-law had twice abandoned the entire family for several weeks, the first time in 1938 when she went to Europe to try to rescue relatives from the Nazi onslaught. I used to tell Sid that his mother's problem was that she was born fifty years too soon and would have had an easier time in our world.

My mother-in-law's feminist attitude and her unwavering acceptance of me are perhaps best illustrated by an incident that took place one weekend when Sid was in Montreal. She and I were in the living room where she had just told me of meeting an acquaintance of mine on the bus the previous day. From what she said, it was obvious that she had been bragging about me, and that furthermore she had said things that were simply not true. I responded by telling her how angry and embarrassed I was, and Sid entered the room during my harangue. He didn't know what had happened, but he was upset at what he heard me saying, and at his first opportunity he said "Don't talk to my mother that way!" whereupon she turned to me and asked "Since when does he give you orders?"

That year was probably the most difficult of my life, but the insight I developed into Sid's background as a result of living with his family was invaluable. The family was invariably kind and complimentary to me, my sister-in-law Bess became a very good friend, and I was treated very well. However, the home was full of disorder, nobody knew how to manage, and it was hard to remain focused on my studies. I would escape to Ottawa, and I spent a lot of time on campus, but I did barely well enough on my exams to graduate with second class honors in math & physics, where until then I had always had first-class marks.

On his side, I know that Sid had a very hard time when we were with my family. He did not know how to deal with everyone talking at once, people finishing each other's sentences, or feeling free to say something like "Don't be silly" to express a difference of opinion. What he did do very well when we were alone, though, was point out to me how expert all the members of my family were at taking care of themselves in any disagreement, which he sometimes described as "attacking wit   le."

Sid died o   ich cancer after we were married for 48 years,   three months after his condition was diagnose   ough the realization that he was going to die   hrough to me two or three weeks before the d   had enough information to tell us what the pro   was. I'm still living a full and active life, but I've   surprised to find that as time goes on, that hole in my life still hurts as much as ever, sometimes even more.

Sidney O. Kastner in Syracuse Graduate Housing, circa 1955

**Sid and Bernice, dance at their wedding,
June 30th, 1951, Montreal**

7. "You can't be all things to all people"

The launching of the satellite Sputnik by the Soviet Union in October, 1957 had an enormous impact on my life. By then Sid and I had two daughters, two and three years of age, and Sid was well along in his Ph.D. program. We were living in student housing at Syracuse University, where all the women were either working or baby-sitting or both, and I had held a series of rather interesting part-time jobs by exchanging baby-sitting with my neighbors while I tried to decide whether or not I was ready to start serious graduate work myself. At the time of the Sputnik launch I was doing statistical calculations for a group of sociologists at the Veterans' Hospital in Syracuse, and I had already taken two graduate-level courses in Physics.

Suddenly there was a call for more and better-trained teachers of mathematics and science, and the Education Department at Syracuse University offered a "fifth-year program" program that was designed for people like me who had a Bachelor's degree with a strong major (I had two, mathematics and physics) but no formal courses in education. I made inquiries to the local school system and was told that I could have temporary certification and a teaching job at the secondary level as soon as I had taken just two courses: Methods of Teaching Mathematics and the Student Teaching Practicum, and I could take the other courses over a longer time period.

With two young children, and plans to have more children eventually, I realized that this might be a good direction for me to take, since it would allow me to be home with my children in the summers. After thinking about what I would prefer to teach, I decided it would be mathematics, since it was obvious to me that you can't do physics if you don't have the needed mathematics background.

I applied for a teaching assistantship in the mathematics department and was initially turned down because they were "tired of hiring Physics wives" (!!!). However, someone who had been hired decided at the last moment not to come, and I received a telephone call on the Friday before the start of classes asking if I would be able to begin teaching on Monday. I decided it was in my own interest to accept this offer, since I had already registered in both courses that were required for temporary certification.

Now I was suddenly very busy, since I taught two sections of College Algebra as well as taking the Methods of Teaching Mathematics course and doing the student teaching. But the girls were both attending the University's excellent nursery school, we had a network of backup babysitting, Sid had enough flexibility in his schedule to be with them if necessary, and it all worked out.

I was fortunate to be assigned to one of the most effective teachers I have ever known for my Student Teaching Practicum, and it was through this experience that I learned, at the very beginning of my teaching career, that "you can't be all things to all people." Although I have forgotten the name of this wonderful teacher, I have never forgotten how well she was able to discern and deal with the various problems her students experienced in learning mathematics. I was assigned one of her classes for my student teaching, but I always arrived earlier so I could help with the class she had in the time period before mine, because she was doing such interesting things with these students, who were clearly functioning well below their nominal grade 7 level.

I subsequently learned that all the students in this class had behavior problems in their other classes, because frequently one or another of them was called out to visit the Principal's Office. However, in their math class they all worked productively, in pairs or small groups, at tasks they could manage, that were designed to help them master whatever this excellent teacher felt was suitable.

The methods course was taught in seminar fashion by Dr. Robert Davis, who went on to develop the Madison Project at the beginning of what became an era of mathematics curriculum revision, and this project eventually became a part of what evolved into the "New Math." I reported on this class during one of the seminars, and shortly afterwards Dr. Davis attended the class and then began to attend regularly in order to try out, with great success, some of the strategies he went on to develop into the Madison Project after he received funding from the National Science foundation in subsequent years. In fact, the project was named for the school in which my supervising teacher taught, Madison Junior High School.

Most students in the class I taught as well as the class I have just described appreciated that they had a superb teacher, but I was also present at one of the PTA evenings where I heard complaints to and about this teacher, which made me aware that no matter how well you do the job, there will be those who are not satisfied. In my own teaching career, this knowledge was very helpful when I had to deal with criticism from students or parents.

After completing the two initial courses required for temporary certification, I still had my teaching assistantship and so I continued on in the "fifth year program" and was able to complete my Master's Degree in mathematics education before we left Syracuse, and was fully certified as a teacher when Sid accepted a position at the Goddard Space Fight Center in Greenbelt, Maryland.

8. "Where there's a will there's a way"

On giving birth

I was fortunate to have discovered the book *Childbirth Without Fear*, by the British obstetrician Grantly Dick-Read early in my first pregnancy. In this book, Dr. Dick-Read made a compelling case for seeing childbirth as a natural experience that might be accomplished without the need for medication. The benefits to both mother and child were presented clearly, and I was very motivated to try this approach.

My three children were all born in different cities, so that I had to have a different doctor each time. I was careful to look for a doctor in each location who expressed support for natural childbirth, since it certainly was not part of current practice in the 1950s. While I did discover obstetricians who agreed that it was desirable to give birth naturally, it was not until the third and final childbirth experience that I actually had a doctor who gave the method more than lip service. This was all the more surprising, since each of these doctors observed, during the initial examination, that my body is one that is capable of delivering an infant that might be larger than usual, and the largest of my babies only weighed 6 lbs. 3 oz. at birth.

In later years, there was much more support for women who wanted to have a natural childbirth experience, with classes to teach the prospective mother relaxation exercises and the prospective father how to function as a "coach" during the experience. I found the description Dr. Dick-Read provided about the relaxation exercises to be very clear, and I simply followed the instructions as well as I could and felt quite confident that in fact they were helpful.

I got my first hint that my doctor was not quite a believer rather late in that first pregnancy, when I raised the issue of having my husband present during the early part of labor. One of the central tenets of the natural childbirth approach is that the woman in labor should never be left alone, and that the most helpful support can come from her husband. This doctor informed me, however, that in his opinion the fathers are just "in the way," that the labor and delivery rooms in the hospital were on the ninth floor, and the prospective fathers' waiting room was on the seventh floor, and that furthermore he had helped to write that policy. He did go on to tell me that I would, however, never be left alone after being admitted to the hospital in labor.

In spite of this reassurance, once I was actually in the hospital on the third day of what was at first called "false labor" but which simply went on and on, I was in fact left alone for most of the time. As luck would have it, they were very busy that afternoon and evening, and there simply was no nurse free to stay with me, though someone stopped in from time to time to monitor how I was doing. When I finally did feel that I was in fact experiencing a good deal of pain, and I rang the bell for help, the person who responded was one of the cleaning staff. She told me that "they're all in the delivery rooms" but promised to get me some help. After perhaps ten minutes a nurse arrived, and then there was a lot of activity as I was transferred to one of the delivery rooms, and my doctor appeared on the scene.

One of the nurses suggested that I should bear down and push, which did help alleviate the pain, but by that time my doctor had informed me that he was giving me a shot of Demerol for the pain. In retrospect I understood that if I had realized that what I needed to do was to bear down when it got that painful, I probably would not have needed the Demerol. But at least I was fully awake and able to actively participate in giving birth, which I found thrilling.

As it turned out, I had entered the hospital in midafternoon on my birthday, and Judy was born about 20 minutes before midnight, so she arrived just in time for us to have the same birthday.

For the second pregnancy, my doctor used a small maternity hospital for the birthing experience, though again I was told that the policies did not permit the husband to be in the labor room with his wife. But I thought that now that I had some experience – I knew what it felt like to transition from the initial stage of labor to the stage where you have to bear down – I would manage well even if I were again left alone.

However, this time the experience was completely different, in that while the nurses did have the time to monitor the labor room effectively, after a while I found myself engaged in a disagreement with the doctor. My labor was proceeding steadily, although quite slowly. The contractions were very regular, and sufficiently close together to have warranted admission to the hospital, but it did look as though it was again going to take a while.

Out of the blue, it seemed to me, the doctor suggested that he wanted to give me a shot of Demerol. I said that I didn't need it, and his response was that when I did need it, it would be "too late." I told him that I didn't expect to need it, but he persisted. Finally, I gave in – after all, I had had a shot of Demerol when giving birth to Judy and it was still a positive experience, so I decided not to keep on with the argument.

But very shortly after I was given the shot, a contraction began that simply did not stop. I went from being not much more than halfway dilated to the complete birth on a single contraction. Suddenly, they were administering oxygen to me, because the fetal heart was slowing, and when Ruth began to emerge she was quite purple. But she cried before she was fully born and immediately the purple began to fade. I was told that the cord had been trapped between my bones and her head, and since the contraction had not receded, they were administering oxygen to me to maximize what would reach her. I felt as though I could dance away from the delivery room, I was so energized by all that oxygen, but they did wheel me back to my room in the usual way.

I read an article in a newspaper or magazine several months later about the drug called Pitocin that had recently become available to induce labor or to make it more "effective," and I could not help wondering if I had been given Pitocin rather than Demerol in that shot. It seemed that perhaps the doctor had realized that it was likely that we were going to be there all night at the rate my labor was progressing, and he wanted to speed it up a little. Since I did not investigate, I will never know. But I was too busy taking care of my two little girls, only 17 months apart in age; Sid was already planning to go back and finish his graduate work; and I did not have the appetite to pursue legal action if I had discovered that my suspicions were correct.

For my third pregnancy, about four years later, I did find a doctor who really understood what natural childbirth was all about. Of course, by then I had learned how to interview the doctor and ask the right questions. I was already pregnant when we moved to Greenbelt after Sid accepted the position with the Goddard Space Flight Center, and although I did not yet have a driver's license and would have preferred to use one of the local obstetricians, I was not satisfied that any of them understood natural childbirth. But Greenbelt was a good town in which to talk with people and someone recommended Dr. Brew highly. When I spoke with him, I was quite confident that he understood, and indeed he did.

When I went into labor and was admitted to the hospital, Sid was expected to stay with me in the labor room as long as we both wanted this. Dr. Brew came in to let me know that he had been having a very busy day, and that he was going to rest in a nearby room, but he was to be sent for as soon as I felt this was necessary. When I felt the transition, I asked Sid to go find the nurse so that we could inform Dr. Brew. Sid came back with the nurse, who stood at the doorway and looked at me and said "Oh, no, it can't be, she's not in enough distress." I suggested that she needed to examine me, and when she did everything got very busy.

I was wheeled to the delivery room, and Dr. Brew came in right away. He seated Sid at my head, where he could hold my hand but not have to be exposed to the real action, though there was a mirror so I could see what was happening, as could Sid if he wanted to. Sid told me later that he felt squeamish enough not to look, though he was as thrilled as I was when Joel was born and we heard his first cry. I think I can say that this birthing experience was probably the high point of my life. I was on an emotional "high" for months afterwards and never experienced any post-partum depression, even though we were living in rather small quarters with three young children.

A few years ago, I read an article in a newspaper or magazine that claimed that the female orgasm has no purpose. I wondered if this is because so few women have ever given birth naturally. My own experience was that when I finally was permitted to give birth in this way, with my husband holding me, it could best be described as a fantastic orgasm. Perhaps the "purpose" of the female orgasm is connected with giving birth, something that has been distorted beyond recognition in modern life.

9. "A watched pot never boils"

I heard this expression a lot when I was growing up, but it was never in the context of cooking – it was used to let us know that if we were waiting for something to happen it was best to pass the time by doing something else. But it does conjure up an image of the kitchen.

My mother was wonderful cook, and so was my grandmother when she took over the kitchen after she came to live with us. Neither of them used cookbooks or recipes, and they were both capable of adjusting to the conditions in which the cooking had to take place. When I was very young, my mother didn't bake, because she didn't have a reliable oven, but she made her own doughnuts, since these were fried on the stovetop. When we spent our summers in the country, my mother and later my grandmother cooked and baked all kinds of good things on the wood-burning stove, often using ingredients that were in season on the farm.

My brother, sister, and I all enjoy cooking and we do it for recreation as well as necessity. In fact, during the last year that I spent teaching mathematics at the junior high school level before I entered the Ph.D. program at the University of Maryland, I found myself cooking as an antidote to the tremendous frustration of my job. My daughters must have been in grades 5 and 6 at that time, and my son in kindergarten. I really loved teaching at the junior high school level, it was thrilling to see how excited the students would get when we tackled the big ideas that underlie the techniques that form the mainstay of mathematics education.

I saw five classes every day, and there were between 30 and 34 students in each class. The school in which I taught had an "ability grouping" policy, so that theoretically all the students in each class were capable of learning at the same pace. This might have worked better if the groups had been smaller, but I found a wide range of backgrounds and levels of understanding of prerequisite material in these supposedly uniform classes, and there was never enough time, either at school or at home, to do the required planning nor was it possible to find enough classroom time to meet individual needs.

In general, I would get a great deal of satisfaction when I could serve a good dinner that my family enjoyed, and that particular year it became even more important. By then I knew some strategies that worked well, so that I had a repertoire of meals that didn't take very long to prepare, which I combined with a weekend practice of stock-piling such family favorites as my home-made spaghetti sauce in the freezer, or cooking a large pot roast or stew that only had to be reheated a couple of days later. We did not have a microwave at that time, but I did have a well-equipped kitchen.

My children all enjoyed cooking as well. There was one summer when both girls were in high school and had been unable to find a summer job. I had always avoided teaching in the summer, but that year I took on an experimental course, and I was teaching every weekday for six weeks. Judy and Ruth wanted to earn money by selling baked goods, and since I was going to be on campus for six or seven hours at a stretch, I turned the kitchen over to them, and they created "Kastner's Kitchen." They put notices up in places like the local supermarket and the recreation center and took orders for home-made bread such as whole wheat, pumpernickel, and white; quick breads such as banana and pumpkin bread, cookies and brownies.

Unfortunately, though, their business advisor (it was me) should have advised them to set a higher price for their products! The procedure we used was to double the cost of the ingredients, but we should have tripled it. In spite of the fact that they worked hard for not much money, I thought it was a successful venture. And, of course, the rest of the family enjoyed all the fresh bread and baked goods they managed to make available for our own consumption.

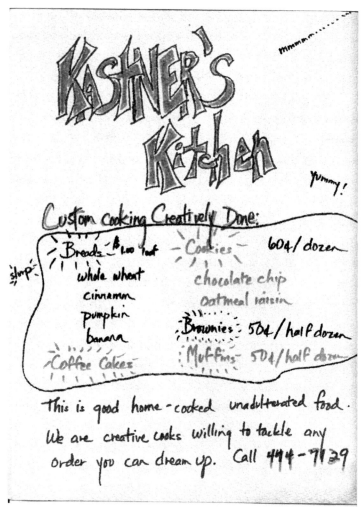

Flyer for Kastner's Kitchen

10. "Nothing ventured, nothing gained"

Although I left public school teaching because I could not find enough time to do the job to my own satisfaction and also manage my family life, it seemed to me that, with my children now all in school, I did have enough time to do something less demanding, and I decided to return to graduate school to begin a Ph.D. program in mathematics. On the premise of "nothing ventured, nothing gained" I applied to the graduate program at the University of Maryland, and even obtained a teaching assistantship so that I did not have to pay tuition, and earned a stipend as well.

I did manage to take two graduate-level mathematics courses each semester and also handle the responsibilities of the teaching assistantship, once I accepted the idea that I was not going to be able to give my studies enough time to achieve grades above the minimum required for survival. I remember telling myself that the choice was either to go to graduate school and not do well or to give up the idea of graduate school for a long time, and therefore it would be better to go and not worry about earning less than stellar grades.

About half-way through the second semester, I had a meeting with my advisor to plan the program for my second year, and he urged me to enroll in three courses each semester in the following year. I told him that I was barely keeping my head above water as it was, and there was no way I would be able to manage a bigger load, and his response was to advise me to spend less time on my teaching responsibilities. It was this piece of advice that made me realize that I was more interested in being a teacher than a mathematician, and I immediately made an appointment with an advisor in the Education Department at the university, after which I transferred to the Mathematics Education Ph.D. program.

Now everything became even more manageable, because I was offered a position as an Instructor, and there was no requirement for taking courses, although the tuition was remitted if I did. So I continued with my own studies, but in some semesters I only enrolled in one course, and I was able to get a lot more satisfaction when I could master the material better.

What was even more gratifying was that I came under the influence of a master pedagogue named Helen Garstens. While I never formally took a course that she taught, she became my mentor, and I feel I learned more about teaching mathematics from Helen than anyone before or since. She had designed the courses for prospective elementary school teachers that I had been hired to teach, and it was in her supervision of what I did in teaching these courses that she shared her expertise in creating successful learning experiences.

Helen's highest degree was a Master's degree, but she had served as the mathematics supervisor for one of the school systems in Virginia, and had received much recognition for her professional development programs for Mathematics teachers, and held a joint appointment in Mathematics and Education. However it was her lack of a Ph.D. that eventually led to an incident that provoked her into taking an early retirement. I never found out what actually took place, even though I continued to see her over the years after she left. I know she felt that she had accomplished her own goals in the design of the courses I taught, and she could also see the "handwriting on the wall" with respect to the eventual lowering of the mathematics course requirements for elementary school teachers.

My connection with the Mathematics Education faculty at the University of Maryland, and the education I received there, was most inspiring. During those years I felt that I was privileged beyond measure. While I was earning a modest income, Sid was the breadwinner and any income I brought in made our life easier but I felt no pressure to continue unless I was getting something beneficial for myself from the experience. During those years I had the exhilarating feeling that I had it all – a supportive husband, wonderful children, and the opportunity to develop my own interests in a very satisfying way.

The Graduate Committee in the faculty of Education welcomed my proposal that I should be allowed to take some courses that would not normally be part of a program like mine when I decided that I wanted to learn about exciting new research in biophysics, and to bring myself up to date in modern physics by taking a Quantum Physics class. With the active support of my dissertation advisor, I was also successful in getting the department to accept a research proposal that was based on curriculum development rather than statistical research. My doctoral thesis was based on the development of a course for high school teachers in which the teachers learned a great variety of interesting applications of the mathematics they taught in high school. Since I had considerable experience in statistics, I also designed a statistical study to establish my credibility in this kind of research. This study was intended to investigate whether open-book testing was meaningful, but I was never able to get enough support to actually carry out the study.

Eventually, the National Council of Teachers of Mathematics (NCTM) published the book I wrote to make the applications material available to a wider audience, *Applications of Secondary School Mathematics*. Publication of this book led to my receiving a commission from NASA for another book, the second edition of *Space Mathematics, A Resource for Teachers*.

A big factor in my successful attempts to design my own graduate program was that I didn't feel it would matter very much if I never completed my Ph.D. I knew that I was in a field where demand was high, and that I already had the credentials that would allow me to teach mathematics in some capacity. In the end, the attainment of the degree made a big difference to my career, but I was glad that I believed it wouldn't matter while I was in the process of getting it, since it was this belief that made me bold enough to shape the path I took to the goal.

Bernice After Her Ph.D Graduation Ceremony

11. "A thing of beauty is a joy forever"

The Diamond Ring Effect

One of the most profound experiences of my life occurred in March of 1970, when Sid took the family to Virginia Beach to see a total solar eclipse that was going to take place close enough to make the trip feasible. Although I had been well briefed on what to expect, the experience itself was too dramatic and awe-inspiring for any possible preparation.

Sid had prepared for this trip by building a special piece of equipment to take pictures. He constructed a long "tube" with a lens at one end and a film holder at the other. The tube was made of four boards, so it was square rather than round, and three people were needed in order to take each photograph, because the person who loaded the film magazine was too far away to open the shutter of the lens, and it was also necessary to load a new film magazine for each picture.

As a NASA employee, Sid had permission to use

the site that the Goddard Space Flight Center had reserved in order to make official observations and measurements of the event. Our family group provided a bit of comic relief to the people making the official measurements, because of the home-made equipment we were using. Sid carefully oriented the long box that served as the camera. What he used to prop it into position and keep it there was a kitchen stool that he had made from the high chair our children had used when they were very young.

He had organized his team and explained carefully what we were to do: Joel passed each film magazine to me, I inserted it into the film holder, Sid opened and shut the lens cover, then on his signal I removed the exposed film and inserted the new one that Joel passed to me. We began with a loaded camera, and once we were close to totality we began to take pictures. As I recall we were able to expose perhaps six films while the moon was passing in front of the sun.

Meanwhile, I was trying to take in all that was happening, and it was truly incredible. It began to get darker and cooler, and the birds started twittering louder and louder. Then, suddenly, the shadow bands – alternating dark and light bands -- were rushing along the ground, and then it got very dark and the birds were silent. After a very short time, it began to get light again, and the birds again got noisy. Meanwhile I was loading and unloading the film cartridges on signal. As the daylight slowly returned to normal, I was wishing I could relive it – it was all over too quickly. I remember thinking that if I were rich, I would become an eclipse-chaser and travel to each location where a solar eclipse was to happen. Even though I had been provided with a lot of information, and I knew the technical explanation for the phenomenon, the actual experience came as a huge emotional jolt, somehow, and I wanted to experience it again.

Since it was about a four hour drive from Greenbelt to Virginia Beach, we had arranged to stay in a motel and drive home the next day. Once we had settled in at the motel, Sid began the process of developing the Polaroid films to see if our picture-taking efforts had been successful. How exciting it was when we reached the picture that showed the solar corona, and even more so once he had developed the one that showed the "diamond ring effect" when the first bit of sunlight reaches out from behind the moon. All of us were jumping up and down with excitement.

My daughter Judy later wrote a poem that expressed her experience of the eclipse as well as her memories of growing up stargazing with her father, Sid. This poem appeared in the journal "Science '82"; it is reprinted on the following page.

The two pictures I have just described hang next to the doorway in my home. I see them whenever I approach the door. In a sense, then, I do relive the experience all the time, even though I never have managed to actually be at another solar eclipse.

Waiting

--by Judith Skillman

His thesis was crystals
compact enough to live
for weeks on sunlight.
He showed us constellations
while we slept on pillows
under meteor showers,
waiting for supernovas.
Or did headstands
on wet grass under the moon's
partial eclipse, pink craters
that ached to be beautiful.

Once in Virginia the sun
performed for him,
with shadow waves,
the threat of total blindness,
the diamond ring effect.
Always his telescope,
the extension of myopia,
was poised under the stars
he owned, the red and the blue,
the Horsehead Nebula,
the Seven Sisters.

We are still waiting
under starless nights for bright
and focused points of light
with names like Ganymede, Io,

and Cassiopeia,
to count more moons,
to fall asleep under the influence
of a different gravity.

**Sid's photo of the total lunar eclipse,
Virginia Beach, March, 1970**

12. "You can curse the darkness or you can light a candle"

I don't think I ever heard this at home – I think I read it somewhere, but it fit naturally into the way I had been raised. It was never any use to complain about something you didn't like in your life, you were sure to be told to snap out of it. The thing to do if you didn't like something and you couldn't just ignore it was to fix it. Sometimes I discovered that in fact I couldn't fix it, but at least I did learn something by trying.

It was this world-view that got me involved in the bargaining between faculty and administration at the community college. There had been conflicts over how much influence the faculty had with respect to such issues as curriculum and hiring of new faculty, and the Faculty Association had succeeded in obtaining special legislation from the Maryland State Legislature to permit it to bargain with the administration, hitherto forbidden since the College was publicly funded.

I joined the effort as part of my philosophy of trying to fix a problem rather than simply complain about it, and the group asked me to take on the role of chief negotiator, which I accepted. I was the only one on our side who was permitted to talk at the table, and the chief negotiator for the administration was an experienced lawyer, but my team was happy with my work. Apparently this was because I was oblivious to the barbs and needles they told me the lawyer was directing my way. There were times when he said things that appeared to me to be non-sequiturs or simply not relevant, but I never recognized that he was trying to get a rise out of me, and when we would break to caucus, they would say something admiring about how I'd "kept my cool" when the fact was I hadn't even detected that I was supposed to be upset.

At times when the lawyer was obviously stalling or unwilling to address the issues of concern, my team asked me to bring my knitting to the table. I always had it with me to help pass the time when we were waiting for the other side's caucus to end, and when I did bring it to the table, it infuriated the lawyer. But I calmly told him that I would put it away as soon as he stopped wasting my time, and this became an effective strategy.

The hardest thing I had to do as the chief negotiator was to address an angry meeting of our faculty. It was clear that the lawyer was skilled at stalling, and there were many among the faculty who began talking about a strike. We could just see the beginnings of some movement when this meeting took place, and I made a plea to the attendees to give us another couple of weeks before taking such a drastic step. We received a very strong vote to hold off, and I received a lot of applause. I came away from that meeting feeling that it might be easy to be a demagogue, but then I realized that in fact they didn't really want to strike, they just wanted to see progress, and we did succeed in making some progress in the next few weeks.

I did not remain as the chief negotiator until the conclusion of the bargaining, because I had been successful in my application to the NSF for a year of professional development so that I could become computer-literate, and since it had taken so long to begin to make progress, the contract negotiations were not finished until after I was on leave.

One of the things I learned rather late in life, that came out of my efforts to "fix" one problem or another, is that the only behavior I can change is my own. This is a most important lesson, and I wished I had learned it earlier, but "better late than never" is another aphorism that applies here. The really interesting aspect of this lesson is that when we realize that we can't get someone else to change, and that the only way to deal with an uncomfortable situation is to figure out how to change our own part in the picture, it often happens that the other person reacts by changing his or her behavior as well.

Sophie Kastner wearing the hat and sweater Bernice knit for her

13. "Don't look a gift horse in the mouth"

--Judith Skillman

When I first got enough distance to think back on my childhood, I realized that my parents were very poor when Ruth and I were born, and even five and half years later when Joel, the longed-for firstborn Jewish son, was born. There are two parts to this poverty that stand out for me. One is the fact that I never felt poor, even when we were living in a two bedroom, thin-walled townhouse, three kids in one room and two parents in the room next to it. Secondly, it was made clear to me from an early age that what is important in life is not appearances; rather it is what one does with one's life that counts.

This lesson was driven home again and again by both my mother and father. My father was a solar physicist at Goddard Space Flight Center, one of the NASA facilities, and my mother worked various jobs as a teacher, always full-time. I wasn't fully aware that part of that time she was in school getting her PhD, because I was too busy growing up and going to college myself, but I suppose that her receiving her PhD in Mathematics Education when I got my B.A. in English in 1976 made it very clear that she'd worked hard and long to achieve her personal goals in the field of education, and that education is extremely important, perhaps more important than owning a fancy house.

Music was very much a part of the Kastner family while I was growing up. My sister Ruth and I played violin under the tutelage of Dr. Berman, who was by all accounts an excellent musician, but had a way of making me feel bad. He said "That stinks," or used other colorful expressions to urge us to practice more. He was an excellent violinist, but perhaps not the best teacher.

I did take a one on one class from Dr. Berman at the University of Maryland when I fancied I might major in music one semester, this idea having come to me sometime after Psychology, Fine Art, and later, Modern Dance; and before French film studies. I finally settled for a B.A. English, and went on to get an M.A. in English Literature with an emphasis in creative writing, as the terminal M.F.A degree didn't exist in 1983.

In any case, my renewed studies of the violin under Dr. Berman should perhaps have made clear to me that I am too shy to be a violinist. It took three more decades to figure that one out. I did, however, profit from the study of music in many ways. Of all the arts it is perhaps the least tangible. Much like writing, however, what is produced can be copied and distributed, and certainly music is the universal language for feelings. But musicians are often underpaid. Many don't succeed at their art for the same reason that poets and writers don't succeed: the competition is intense.

I remember my mother receiving, for her birthday, a harpsichord kit. She and my father sent away for it, and it came, and they put it together. It was an exquisite instrument and stood in the living room for two or three years. The endeavor of putting the kit together and having an actual harpsichord in the house generated the kind of excitement that still accompanies my favorite activities—writing poems and making stained glass windows. When I think back to growing up in my original family, it is that honoring of discovery, art, and creativity—that nurturing of the spirit, that impresses me the most about my mother and father. While my brother and sister have the gift of analytic thinking that makes the sciences tangible and accessible, I do not. But there was never any disappointment expressed about this. Rather, I was encouraged to explore the strong interests I had. I was a voracious reader and, as a teenager, I read Barth, Tolkien, Salinger, Faulkner, Hemingway, Roth, Michener, Kate Chopin—in short, anything and everything I could get my hands on. Most of my literature came from the Greenbelt Library. We didn't buy books, but I got some at second-hand shops.

This brings me to the gist of "Don't look a gift horse in the mouth" and its meaning for me as an adult in an upper middle-class income bracket, looking back on a lower middle-class childhood. Second-hand goods were commonplace in my house. Money was spent on observatory building (my father was an amateur astronomer and took amazing photos of the sky with his own, hand-ground mirror and twelve inch telescope with clock drive—a whole other story) and violin lessons, and some teak furniture. But overall, money was not used for clothing, frills, or anything that wasn't useful in the sense of being utilitarian as well as necessary for daily life.

I remember one summer my sister Ruth, who was "into" pottery, wanted a kiln. The next thing I knew, she had a whole ceramics studio on our glassed in porch downstairs, complete with a potter's wheel, a kiln, various glazes, and a huge bag of clay. I was envious, and tried my hand at it, as in fact I would do again many years later in my thirties when I took a pottery class at a local community college. I found I enjoyed the process, but it wasn't my niche. Her studio was proof, however, that there was simply no ceiling to which our parents would not go to support the creative urge. They would not, however, have a wet bar, invest in the stock market, or buy a new car.

This was in stark contrast to many of my friends, who had new clothes and lots of "stuff." If I wanted a skirt, I would buy the fabric and the pattern, and make the skirt in an evening so I could wear it the next day. My mother, though she worked full time, always had her sewing projects out on the dining room table on week ends, and she cooked up a storm. Things were home-made in the best sense of the word—made by one's own two hands, and with a sense of pride and accomplishment that rivaled the best-dressed girls, those who knew how to use make up and do their hair.

It was a unique experience to grow up with such a variety of creative "preoccupations." I have no doubt that it has played a strong role in my choice of occupation. I am a poet, and that brings in almost no money. I teach for two universities part-time to have an income, but I'm lucky in that my husband has chosen to be the breadwinner for our family. His knack lies in that arena. Mine does not. Due to the respect and dignity the arts held for my parents while I was growing up, I have never felt undermined in my quest for the muse. This thirty-year quest is not based on ambition, although it can't be completely divorced from a certain tenacity and desire for recognition. But writing poems is simply something I do. The fact that it brings in little or no money doesn't usually trouble me unless I happen to get into a self-pity mode. Then I remember how valuable the lessons were, growing up in the Kastner household—"Don't look a gift horse in the mouth."

This gift, as I think about it now, well into middle age, represents the act of creativity, the metaphoric horse. Within this idiom lie the horse's teeth, which are not necessarily sound. The horse, however, is real; it occupies space, wanders ceaselessly around the grounds prepared for it by solitude and reflection, trots in and out of one's life, and when it comes and stands before me, hungry to be taken in, I accept this gift with open arms and am grateful it was given to me while I was young. Even more, I am thankful that no one ever told me, when I was wont to spend whole days glued to a book, or to try a different instrument such as the flute or the guitar or the viola de gamba, "No, you can't do that, it's frivolous." Rather, I was encouraged to experiment in any and all kinds of ways with the creative force that rejuvenates one's deepest self, and, even while lying dormant at times, gives one a "raison d'etre."

14. "Little children, little problems, big children, big problems"

Kleyne kinder, kleyne tsures;
groise kinder, groise tsures

My mother must have said this to me for the first time when our girls were in high school. By this time my parents were retired and spending three or four months in Miami Beach each winter. My mother had asthma and my father had arthritis, and they needed to get away from the severe Montreal winters. They preferred to fly directly between Montreal and Miami, but occasionally they would stay with us for a week or two, usually on their way back to Montreal.

My mother's comment came as our older children were entering adolescence and the surrounding society seemed very threatening, with the prevalence of drugs, the growing emphasis on sexual promiscuity, and the unrest about Vietnam, to name the biggest worries. Although they came through and went on to higher education, our children's high school years were very difficult. Joel was the lucky one who was able to avoid the worst of it, because by the time he reached high school I was teaching at the Community College in the adjacent county, and we had a number of high school students taking calculus at the college while concurrently enrolled in high school. My inquiries regarding whether he could do something similar, and the subsequent placement testing that was part of Prince Georges Community College's admissions process, resulted in his acceptance so that he attended the college instead of the last two years of high school.

For Judy and Ruth, though, those years were terrible. What made matters even worse was that it took us a long time to realize just how bad the situation was. The school was brand new the year that Judy started there, but from the day it opened it was overcrowded. One day I received a telephone call from one of Judy's teachers who wanted me to know that Judy was late for every class. When I told Judy about this conversation, she said that in the transitions between classes the hallways were so packed with tall students – Judy is relatively short – that not only couldn't she see where she was going, but she felt that she could easily be trampled. Her solution was to wait in the nearest girls' bathroom until the crowds subsided, and this made her late for class.

At that time I was working on my Ph.D. program in Education at the University of Maryland and I had heard about the great hopes for this school. The new Principal had been an excellent teacher, but he proved to be an ineffectual administrator. However, it's not entirely fair to blame him because he too was a victim of a system operating under the misguided belief that "bigger is better" for a high school, and of the problems that arose from the local history of weak school and community racial integration.

That school went from bad to worse, and in the one year that Joel spent in it, he experienced an unbelievable amount of chaos. At one point, for example, the fire department had to come once or twice a week while all the students stood outside because apparently some boys had learned how to create an automatic fire alarm by setting fire to a roll of toilet paper in the bathroom.

I was also slow to understand what my children were going through because my own high school experience had been so good. Whereas in Maryland we lived in the suburbs, I grew up in a city where everyone walked to school, or used public transportation if the walk was too long. Our school was a community as well as a place to learn. Almost everyone joined the choir, we had an excellent music teacher, Mr. Herbert, and we gave a "Christmas Concert" each year that was reviewed by the music critic for the Montreal *Star*, the major newspaper at the time. An example of Mr. Herbert's wisdom was that he was well aware that 97% of the student body was Jewish – the school was located in the Jewish ghetto – and we sang Oratorio music with Old Testament content. The closest we came to a Christmas Carol at the "Christmas Concert" was *Good King Wenceslas*.

There was tremendous school spirit at Baron Byng. I attended the class reunion 50 years after graduation, and the turnout was very high, attracting graduates from far and wide. I was class president for all four years and captain of the basketball team for two years. Our basketball team did not win a lot of games, but there was a lot of enthusiasm. I also played badminton, which meant going to the school on Saturday mornings. I was not a very good badminton player, but I did get on the team that competed with other schools, as an alternate.

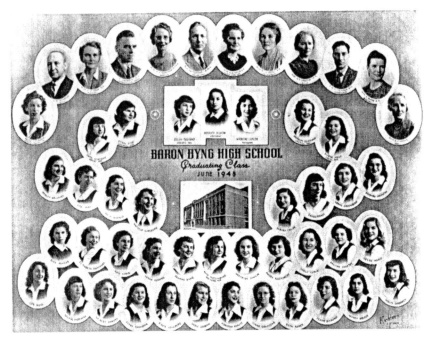

Bernice featured in the center above the
school name, as class president

Photo of "Room 11" 50th reunion for Baron Byng High School

15. "April showers bring May flowers"

--Ruth Kastner

I remember my mother often saying this proverb with a bit of a smile, in her ever-optimistic way. When we were growing up, she would always point out to us the "silver lining" in whatever cloud might be hanging over us at any given time. Misfortune or difficulties were always, to her, either an opportunity to overcome and achieve something or a necessary ingredient in an as-yet-unseen "big picture" that would bring happiness in the end.

In retrospect, it seems as though my sister Judy and I often tended to feel daunted and discouraged by circumstances more easily than Mom did. How much of that was due to the very different culture and environment we grew up in, and how much to innate genetics, I will never know. But it must have been a bit frustrating for her to see us so easily "brought down" by things. However, for the most part she would respond to our discouragement by, in the spirit of this proverb, gently urging us to be patient and have confidence that things would work out for the best.

Along with this proverb comes the memory of when Judy and I were taking ballet lessons (we must have been only 6 and 7), we were preparing for a show that was to include a performance of the song "April Showers". The lyrics went something like:

"Though April showers
May come your way
They bring the flowers
That bloom in May....
So keep on looking for the bluebird
And listening for his song
Whenever April showers come along."

We were supposed to learn to sing this song, which Mom knew, but she said that she wasn't a good singer and that if she taught it to us, we'd learn it wrong. She tried her best, and laughed a great deal about how "flat" she was singing, but I don't really think she was that far off!

As I've grown older, I've often thought of Mom's "make the best of things" attitude, and the wisdom contained in this proverb with its instruction of optimistic patience. It is a very different approach to life than I had for much of my earlier years and adolescence, which were marked by pessimism and often, in retrospect, simple self-indulgence and self-pity. I guess Mom made her optimism look so easy and effortless that it never occurred to me that sometimes one might need to consciously work at "looking for the bright side" of things, instead of dwelling on the darkness. Perhaps this comes more easily to some people than to others, but with some effort and application, it has proved to me to be a pragmatic and effective way to negotiate life's darker aspects.

16. "The only constant in life is change"

By 1980 Sid had become increasingly unhappy in his work at NASA, as the agency moved inexorably toward a "privatization" model. He would frequently observe that he was a scientist and not a manager, as his duties evolved to include much more management and much less science. Meanwhile, I was having my own difficulties just living in Maryland, since it was clearly unwise for me to drive a car, given that it was impossible to predict when one of my brief –but severe -- episodes of "benign positional vertigo" would occur. We had investigated moving out of Greenbelt to another suburb of Washington, or the city itself, that would be better served by public transportation, but it was clear to both of us that we would not be comfortable living anywhere but in Greenbelt if we lived in Maryland.

We began to talk about moving away entirely, even

about returning to Canada to live. We had visited Myer and Peggy in Vancouver many years earlier when we had traveled west across the US and east across Canada with the family by train, and in the summer of 1981 we decided to go back for another visit on our own. A few months later, NASA was ordered to reduce its staff, and Sid discovered that as one of the first employees of the Goddard Space Flight Center, he was eligible to apply for early retirement, although he was only 55 years old.

We proceeded to investigate employment possibilities, and I responded to an advertisement for a "Laboratory Instructor" position at Simon Fraser University that I had seen advertised in the Vancouver Sun when we visited. I also sent letters to most of the community colleges, since I was then employed by Montgomery College in Maryland. Sid spoke to some people in physics and in astronomy at the University of British Columbia, and it appeared that he had a good chance of getting some consulting work from a proposed joint project among Canada, Australia, and the United States, called "Starlab."

Sid had a meeting with one of the retirement counselors at Goddard, and was quite disappointed with the income he could expect if he sought the early retirement. However, he was even more disappointed with the atmosphere in which he worked. He was in the Solar Physics Branch, and the experiment his group had been working on for over a year, which had been scheduled on the next space shuttle flight, was suddenly cancelled to make room for a secret mission that could only have been military in nature. Although his own work became even more important to the group – as a theoretician, he was always able to "milk" existing data gathered in previous experiments for further results that provided new publications for his colleagues as well as himself – he found the widespread depression among his coworkers intolerable.

Judy and Ruth were married by that time; Judy and Tom had two children, Lisa and Drew, aged 4 and 2, and Tom was working for one of the small computer software development companies in the Washington area. Ruth and Chuck had also married, and Chuck had a job in engineering with one of the contractors at Goddard, while Ruth, with her degree in Music Education from the Peabody Conservatory, had not found satisfactory employment and had started studying Physics at the University of Maryland. Joel had completed a Bachelor's degree in Physics, and was working as a jazz musician in the Washington area. We had our whole family living in Greenbelt, but even so, we decided that we would make the move to Vancouver.

We had not anticipated the reactions of our daughters' spouses when we told them of our plans to move to Vancouver. Tom's parents had moved to Sequim, on the Olympic Peninsula in Washington State a couple of years earlier, when his Dad had retired, and his reaction was one of delight: "That's it, we were going to move to the west coast sooner or later, we'll do it now."

Chuck, on the other hand, was shocked and upset. He said "I thought you loved me, how can you think of going so far away?" It was only then that we understood the differences between his world-view and our own. Sid and I had both come from backgrounds where neither we, nor our parents, nor their parents had the experience that successive generations grew up in the same place – we were the quintessential "wandering Jews." In Chuck's family, successive generations remained close to their origins, perhaps moving as far away as the next State, but certainly no farther. As well, Ruth and Chuck had met at the Conservatory, and we had spent many evenings where Sid and Judy joined them in making music, an activity treasured by all, including me – the listener.

However, Both Sid and I were sufficiently unhappy about our respective problems that we did proceed to plan the move; this became even more appealing when we learned that I had been awarded the Laboratory Instructor position at Simon Fraser University, and we would not have to depend only on Sid's retirement income. We sold our Greenbelt house and the two old cars we had at that time, which we didn't feel were reliable enough to drive across the country, arranged to send some of our furniture and belongings west, and went through the monumental task of disposing of everything else.

I found that my new job and the lifestyle and climate in Vancouver to be most congenial. The Mathematics Department at Simon Fraser University was open to new ideas – indeed, the creation of the position for which I had been hired was in response to perceived problems in the previous system of instruction – and it was always clear to me that I could feel free to raise any pedagogical issues I thought were important. My background and experience were well suited to the demands of the job, and I found my relationship to the students to be very satisfying, since I was perceived as someone who was there to help them.

I was in charge of a "workshop" that supported the precalculus course and the mathematics course for prospective elementary school teachers. I had a staff of graduate students, and we were responsible for the marking of homework and exams, as well as providing individual help to students in the courses. I found it necessary to train these graduate students to understand the difference between tutoring and lecturing, and I also had to organize the work to ensure that the staffing was adequate at the busy times, the marking was fair, and the graduate students were not overloaded. I was also responsible for the record-keeping in these large classes.

Although we lived in the western part of the city and it took me over an hour to get to Simon Fraser University, which is located at the top of Burnaby Mountain, the public transportation system functioned well and I was able to work or knit while traveling. People in Vancouver do complain a lot about all the rain, but I found it easier to deal with the rain than the extremes of heat and cold in the east. About a year into our Vancouver residency we bought a house, and I did think that we were settled.

Sid, however, became more and more unhappy. The "Starlab" project was abandoned by the Canadian government a few months after our arrival, and neither the Physics department nor the Astronomy department at the University of British Columbia had a suitable position, even part-time, for Sid. The Physics Department did provide him with a desk in an appropriate lab, as well as computing and library privileges, but Sid felt he had no identity in his new setting. He had always had many hobbies and interests, and he did some research on his own and even did some collaborating with his former colleagues at Goddard, but he found that these were not sufficient. He was clearly not ready to be retired.

After we had lived in Vancouver for three years, Ruth became pregnant for the second time. Her first daughter, Wendy, was born a year and a half after we moved, and she had not had an easy pregnancy. Judy and Tom were then living in Seattle, having moved west when we did. I decided to take a leave of absence so that we could come back to Greenbelt and be able to help her when the second child was born. Sid was welcomed by his former colleagues and hired to do research through one of the Goddard contractors, and I was offered a visiting position in Mathematics Education at the University of Maryland.

Janet was born in October, and Judy had her third child, Jocelyn, the following January, under traumatic conditions that required emergency surgery. I flew to Seattle to help with Judy's family at that time, and when I returned three weeks later, Sid had prepared all the necessary legal documents and was ready to create his own consulting company, Mathematical Science Consultants (MSC inc.), provided I would be willing to be the other half of the team. It had already become clear to me that Sid had no desire to return to Vancouver, and that he was happier than he had been for many years. As a research consultant he was again a scientist rather than a manager, and having his own company would give him even more control over his work. Of course, it is much easier to live with a happy person than with a miserable one, and I willingly signed the documents and took on the very minimal management role in MSC, Inc. I also had some input to the professional work, since Sid and I had always worked together on matters of mutual interest – he would bring mathematical issues to me, and I had used him as a sounding board and source of information when I was developing my material on applications of mathematics.

We had tenants living in our house in Vancouver, and had rented a unit in the Greenbelt Homes Co-op from a family on sabbatical leave in Europe. I was not ready to abandon all thought of returning to Vancouver, but I decided to put off any real decision for another year. I found another visiting position at Towson State College, later renamed Towson University, in a suburb of Baltimore, and extended my leave of absence from Simon Fraser University for another year. We also found a wonderful unit in the Greenbelt Co-op very close to where Ruth and Chuck lived, which we bought. It had a large two-story addition that gave us plenty of space for the company offices, as well as space when our other children visited. By this time Joel and Amy were in graduate school in Los

Angeles, so the family was scattered on both sides of the continent.

During this second year in Maryland, my colleagues at Simon Fraser University let me know that a one-year visiting position in Mathematics Education was going to be available there for the following year, and this presented an intriguing chance to see if Sid and I could have the best of both worlds by dividing our time between Vancouver and Greenbelt. Faculty members at Simon Fraser University teach during two of the three semesters each year, and may spend the third, a research semester, elsewhere. Summers are busy semesters in Education, and it would be easy for me to arrange to teach in the summer and fall, and to spend the spring semester in Maryland.

Our Vancouver house had a one-bedroom "in-law suite" in the basement, which we had kept vacant for our own possible use when we returned to the east. I applied for and was offered the visiting position, and we came back to Vancouver and occupied this suite in June of 1987. Sid stayed for a couple of weeks before returning to work on site at the Goddard Space Flight Center, and it didn't take very long for me to realize that in fact he was not going to spend much time in Vancouver. By the end of October I was ready to accept the reality that my choice was between living in Vancouver and living with my husband, and I chose Sid.

Of course, we spoke regularly by telephone, and although Sid felt we should keep the Vancouver house – it was clear that real estate values were climbing – I argued for selling it, because I felt I needed to make a clean break. It sold quickly, and Sid came to Vancouver at the end of November to help me empty the house. By the end of December we were both living in Green-belt. I was still employed by Simon Fraser University until the end of April, and I had a most interesting spring term at the Mathematical Sciences Education Board (MSEB). MSEB then hired me through the summer, and by fall I had submitted my resignation to Simon Fraser University, and been hired in a full-time position at Towson University, where I had earlier held a visiting position.

Sid and Bernice visit Mount Rainier, September 20, 1998

17. "It's like bringing coals to Newcastle"

--Joel Kastner

My mom's catch-all aphorism to describe an embarrassment of riches – or, as the case may be, an unnecessary or unwarranted excess – confounded me on a subliminal level until I was well into adulthood.

I knew what coal was; it was that jet-black substance piled high on the train cars that would clatter and clang past Dorothy and Julio's house in Cote St. Luc (that easy access to train-watching was one of my cherished memories of visiting Montreal). I also knew all about charcoal, since that meant cookouts on balmy summer evenings in our back yard at 39F Ridge Road and later at (more prosaically named) 123 Northway.

But what were "coals?" I imagined hunks of blackness, but only the vague images of a six-year-old; somewhere between opening up a bag of "briquettes" and dumping a whole coal car's worth. But how much was enough? How many coals were needed to make the analogy work?

I knew on a gut level -- from the way in which my mother used the phrase -- that it had to be *too many*. There were already too many coals. That was it! Clearly, there were already enough, at this "new castle"...a castle that was being built...out of coal?

I realize how blissfully ignorant my own remembrance sounds, in comparison with my sisters' very insightful and deeply analytical descriptions of the turmoil they associate with even my mom's most optimistic sayings. No wonder. As the youngest of the three siblings, I had all the benefits of their experience, without the pain of the trial-and-error that won them that experience. Not only that, but – as they both were at pains to constantly remind me – I had *three* mothers.

Doubtless one, two, or perhaps all three of them must have tried to explain to me that Newcastle was just a gritty city in England where coal was the engine for the local economy. Newcastle had plenty of coal -- indeed they'd had enough since medieval times; so no need for more. It was as simple as that.

Much later in life, despite a less-than-adequate education in world history, I understood this. But it would take many more years before it dawned on me that this expression must have been passed along to my mother via constant repetition by her Liverpool-bred mother, our beloved Bobbie. Spoken repeatedly in 1960s-suburban Greenbelt, it had completely lost its original context.

So I still prefer my not-quite-fully-conjured, young

child's image of a needless delivery of raw materials to build a castle that was already nearing completion; a castle literally taking shape out of formless blackness.

18. "Bit by bit the bowl gets filled"

A bissl un a bissl macht a fulle shissl

A s a depression-era child in an immigrant family, this was a saying that resonated. Nobody had very much money, and, along with my peers, I understood the necessity as well as the value of slowly accumulating the means to achieve a goal. In recent years I've discovered another context for the idea of working towards a goal that has to take a while to achieve, and in this context there is no more important objective: a body that functions well and makes it possible to enjoy life.

By the time I retired from Towson University in Maryland, at the age of 60, I had gained a lot of weight and was leading the typical sedentary, automobile-based lifestyle of North American suburbia. Several health-related issues had become apparent, such as arthritic knees and elevated blood pressure, which I tended to accept as inevitable outcomes of aging. About two years after leaving academia, I found an interesting position at the American Council on Education as the Mathematics Test Specialist for the GED tests, generally recognized as measures equivalent to high school graduation proficiency, and while I was there the Council offered all its employees an opportunity to be tested for physical fitness.

I took advantage of this testing program and learned formally what already had become obvious to me, that my body had very little flexibility or aerobic fitness in addition to the arthritis. By this time it was hard for me to walk more than four or five blocks without feeling pain in both knees, and when I resigned my position at the Council a year or so later I decided to see what I could do to improve my physical functioning. We were living in Greenbelt, Maryland, which has an excellent municipal swimming pool and fitness center, and I signed up for a water exercise class that met three times a week. At first my knees felt even worse, but I was advised to wear a knee brace and to modify the exercises if discomfort persisted.

After a few weeks the pain was gone and I was able to discard the knee brace, and then I saw an article in the health section of the newspaper pointing out that the best treatment for joint problems was to strengthen the muscles that support that joint. I had also made an effort to modify my eating habits and had lost about 20 pounds, in an effort to control my blood pressure without medication other than the traditional "water pill."

After Sid died, I moved to Rochester, New York, where my youngest granchildren were living. My

Maryland grandchildren were teenagers by then and busy with their own lives, while Sam and Sophie were only 7 and 3 years old, respectively, when I moved. There was an excellent water exercise program at the Jewish Community Center there, and I continued to use this activity. After I had been in Rochester for about a year, my blood pressure was still hovering at a level that my doctor considered not quite satisfactory, and she talked about adding another medication. After filling the prescription and reading the information that was provided, I telephoned her and asked about trying a different approach, such as weight training, and she agreed that we could afford to wait a few more months while I tried this.

I now consider my fitness program to be the most important thing I do. After six years of weight training, instead of taking more medication for blood pressure, the dosage of my original medication has been reduced. However, what is even more important is that *bit by bit* my body has gained in strength and flexibility, and I actually feel younger than I did ten years earlier! I can lift and carry with no problem, and I find it much easier to travel than I used to. I had to have major surgery at the age of 73, and everyone – including me – was amazed at how quickly I recovered.

I've also discovered that I'm one of the lucky people who experience an "endorphin high" after strenuous exercise. This makes it easy for me to work as hard as I can during each of the sessions -- I know that the feel-good reward will follow, and it always does.

Bernice with her Greenbelt water exercise class

Afterword

--Judith Skillman
Thanksgiving, November 27, 2008

Anticipating my mother's arrival for Thanksgiving, I begin to realize how much I have to be grateful for. Not only am I now the "Grammy" of twin fraternal one-year old girls, but this year my mom will take charge of the turkey. She is a wonderful cook, and calls herself a "foody"—one who likes to "mess around" with food. The term is rather an understatement. As anyone who has ever tasted Bernice's delicious meals knows, Bernice is a gourmet cook. This in addition to her willingness to listen makes Jocelyn, who is my youngest, very eager to see her Grandma.

At almost 23 years old, having graduated with a degree in Comparative Sociology from the University of Puget Sound, Jocelyn enjoys hearing stories about the arranged marriage my grandfather had. She also relishes hearing about the lives of generations past. Her relationship with Bernice is special, as it is for all of my children and, indeed for all those fortunate enough to live and work with the upbeat, energetic woman who shrugged off the name "Superwoman" in the seventies, but who embodies the stamina necessary to juggle many balls at once.

Indeed, Bernice, that is, Professor Kastner, will be lecturing at Simon Fraser University this coming winter semester, we learn upon reconnecting with my mom. She will use the online curriculum she recently completed and deliver it "live" to some 125 eager students. She is excited about the prospect, and undaunted by the amount of preparation that lies ahead. Her confidence is palpable.

This is where my mother's and my paths diverge. She is a problem-solver by nature. For Bernice, the analytic path divulges its solution given time and patience. There is no use feeling guilt, and she doesn't; likewise there is no sense wasting time worrying, and she doesn't. While I know these things to be rational, no amount of self-talk on my part keeps me safe and serene in this crazy journey we call life. I, therefore, greatly benefit from Bernice's calm reminders—her proverbs, if you will—her nuggets of wisdom on matters that range from the most simple "A watched pot never boils" to the most complex: "Little children, little problems, big children, big problems…" With every passing year her words carry a deeper ring.

My mother writes me today by email that she will buy some new clothes if she "has the patience." This, to me, embodies the values Bernice exudes. Clothes are important, but not excessively so. The frugal nature of

Bernice—"waste not, want not," comes to life not only in her kitchen but in her life style. She does, however, splurge unstintingly on meals out, assistance with college costs and patronage of music and the arts for her children and grand-children.

This coming year, 2009, promises to be an exciting ride for Bernice, who moved in August to her own place in the Prince Charles Cooperative Building on Pine Street. Her elegant, comfortable, well-lighted one-bedroom place contains the "Rogues Gallery" as always. These portraits of Bernice's loved ones have followed her from Maryland to Vancouver, B.C., to Rochester and back to Vancouver. They reveal her intense love of family and speak to the generosity she shows to her own.

In addition to her support of family and friends, Bernice's positive attitude is abundantly clear to strangers who meet her in her daily walks around whatever town she visits. "Your mother seems so happy," the woman at a Mail Plus in my home town said to me some years ago. "Yes, she is," I replied.

Cheerful, wise, and lovely—there you it. You have read the song of her heartstrings, Bernice Bloom Kastner—Professor, music-appreciator, art-lover, mother, grand-mother, great-grandmother—a splendid person in every way.

A Note About Bernice Kastner

Bernice Bloom was born in Montreal in 1931 and attended Mount Royal Elementary School and Baron Byng High School in Montreal. She was the first woman to earn a B.Sc., Honours Mathematics & Physics, at McGill University (1952). Bernice married Sidney O. Kastner in 1951; subsequently they moved to Syracuse, New York where Sid finished his Ph.D. in Physics, and Bernice acquired a Master's degree in Mathematics Education in 1959.

In 1976 she was awarded the Ph.D degree in Mathematics Education from the University of Maryland. Publications include *Applications of Secondary School Mathematics*, 1978, NCTM, and *Space Mathematics, a Resource for Secondary School Teachers*, 1985, NASA. Kastner has traveled abroad to England, Holland, France, Switzerland, and the Czech Republic, and retains dual citizenship in the U.S. and Canada.

The proud mother of three grown children, seven grandchildren, and two great grandchildren, Bernice is an avid concert enthusiast, a highly accomplished knitter, Professor Emerita of Mathematics from Towson University, and is currently a Research Associate at Simon Fraser University in Vancouver, B.C.

Contributing Authors

Ruth E. Kastner began her undergraduate studies at Peabody Institute in Baltimore, earning a B.M.Ed. She subsequently majored in Physics at the University of Maryland, College Park, receiving a B.S. and M.S. in physics before entering the History and Philosophy of Science program of the UMCP Philosophy Department. Kastner completed her Ph.D. in Philosophy in 1999. She currently directs an a cappella choir, "The Byrd Singers," specializing in the sacred music of William Byrd, the English Renaissance composer. Ruthie lives in Greenbelt, Maryland, with her husband Chuck, a hiker and electronics engineer. In addition to singing and playing the piano, Ruthie makes her own wine and enjoys hiking. She and Chuck have two grown daughters: Inen, an artist, and Janet Hagelgans, a musician.

Joel H. Kastner joined the faculty of RIT's Center for

Imaging Science in 1999. After receiving his Ph.D in Astronomy from UCLA in 1990, Kastner spent almost a decade at MIT, first as a postdoctoral fellow at Haystack Radio Observatory, and then as staff scientist at the Chandra X-ray Observatory Science Center. Kastner's research interests involve studies of the life cycles of stars as well as the development of methods to maximize the science return from astronomical imaging systems. He has co-authored nearly 90 articles in the refereed astronomical literature (more than a third of these as first author, including papers appearing in journals such as *Nature* and *Science*) and has been the lead or co-organizer for about a dozen conferences on astronomy and astronomical imaging. Joel lives in Rochester, New York, with his wife Amy Mednick, a professional writer and editor, and their two children Sam and Sophie.

Judith Skillman's tenth book, *Heat Lightning: New and Selected Poems 1986 – 2006,* was published in 2006 by Silverfish Review Press. Skillman is the recipient of grants from the Academy of American Poets, Washington State Arts Commission, The Centrum Foundation, and other arts organizations. Her poems have appeared in over 200 literary journals and anthologies. A writer, editor, and translator, she lives in Kennydale, Washington with her husband Tom. When not teaching or writing, Judith enjoys the company of her three grown children: Alissa, Andrew, and Jocelyn; and her two fraternal-twin grandchildren, Klara June and Hazel Anne Tuininga.

Acknowledgements

Thanks to Thomas L. Skillman for his unstinting technical support, without which the creation of this memoir would not have been possible.

Thanks to Joel H. Kastner, Ruth E. Kastner, and Judith A. Skillman for their contributions.

The poem "Waiting" appeared in Judith Skillman's first book of poems, *Worship of the Visible Spectrum*, Breitenbush Books, 1987.

Cover art: *Glass Bead Horse* by Judith Skillman: This copper foil design incorporates hand-made ceramic beads by Ashley Miller of JAX Stained Glass, Bellevue, Washington. 17 x 17", framed in zinc.

Bernice in 1944

Bernice with her great grandchildren Klara
June and Hazel Anne Tuininga, 2007

LaVergne, TN USA
28 August 2009
156213LV00004B/9/P